THINGS SAID

A Collection of Healing Words

THINGS SAID

A Collection of Healing Words

by

Chanel Nicole Ryan

Second edition 2020.

ISBN: 978-0-9989945-9-8 (Paperback)

Cover design by LKB Designs & Photography
Cover images by Rupa Kapoor
Interior images by Rupa Kapoor & Chanel Nicole Ryan
Book design by Chanel Nicole Ryan and E. Danielle Butler
Edited by Nzadi Amistad

EvyDani Books
hello@evydanibooks.com
www.evydanibooks.com

Chanel Nicole Ryan
Chanel@ChanelNicoleRyan.com
www.ChanelNicoleRyan.com

DEDICATION

To domestic violence survivors globally -
May you emerge from the shadows to live a life in full color

THINGS SAID

Words are things...said, whether expressed through a written word, a spoken word, or an image. This book is a collection of visual and verbal snapshots; it is my way of telling a story. The content is not always nice and neat, but the words are genuine and sincere. People, like so many things in life, are a work in progress. Sometimes, to capture the true beauty of a person, we must observe them in many different lights.

Chanel

I BELIEVE YOU

Silent Witness

Grace extended her hand ...

Because the lady stumbled before she ran

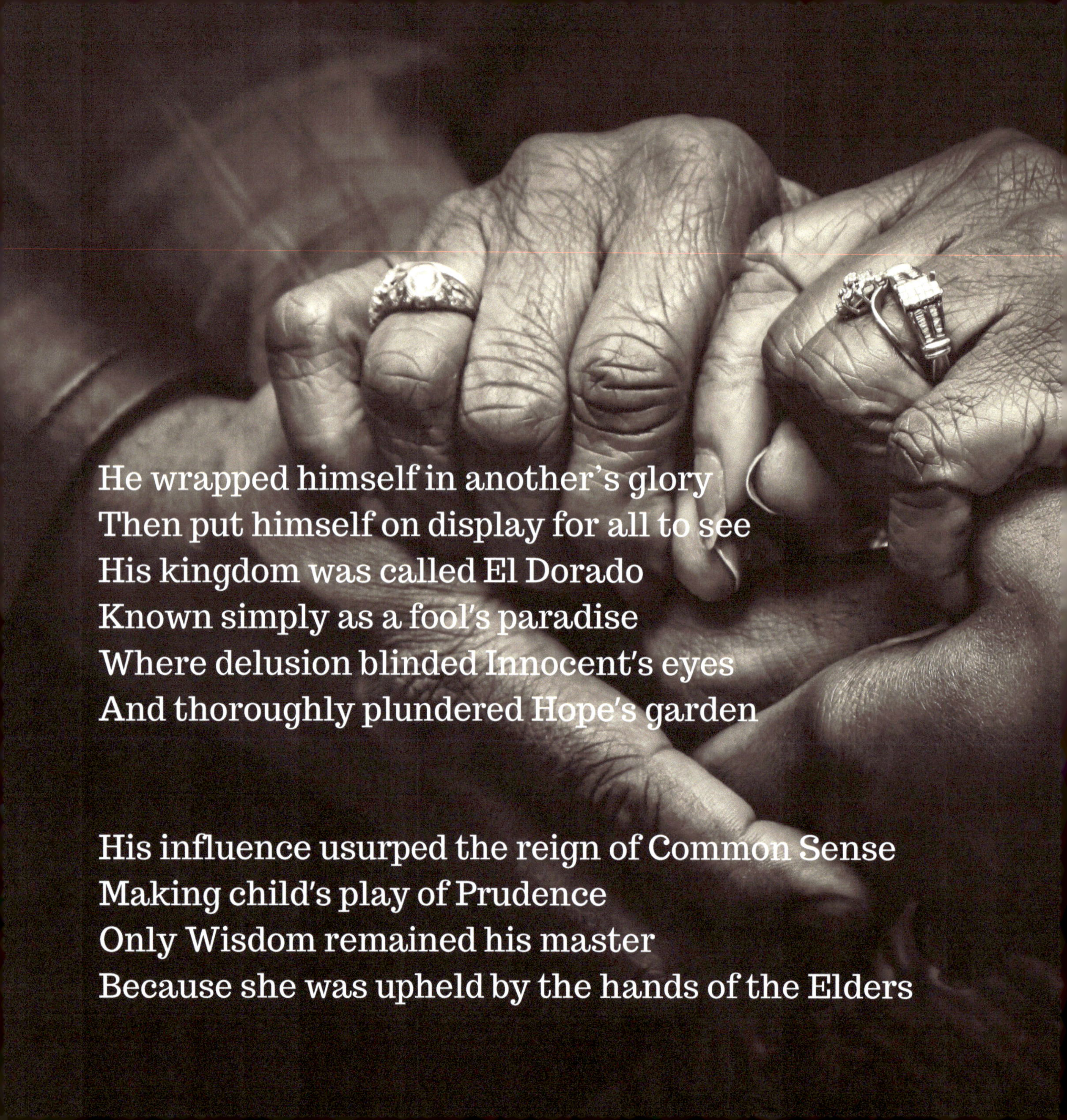

He wrapped himself in another's glory
Then put himself on display for all to see
His kingdom was called El Dorado
Known simply as a fool's paradise
Where delusion blinded Innocent's eyes
And thoroughly plundered Hope's garden

His influence usurped the reign of Common Sense
Making child's play of Prudence
Only Wisdom remained his master
Because she was upheld by the hands of the Elders

I looked to him expecting answers
And was fed a sandwich of silence
Thinly sliced
Between lies and amnesia
And watched years of building
Collapse in a single moment

Maybe if brown
Became black and blue
Or words could leave a visible mark
I would have given the situation
A better name
Instead, I rationalized
Suppressed and denied not knowing
A better reality awaited me

I died a slow and painful death
Just like an oak
Strangled by mistletoe

Circuit

Negativity insisted she explode
Never finding a way to channel positive energy

Standing at the cliff ready to jump
A voice held one hand
While placing a pen in the other
Granting hopeless the chance
To discover her reason for being

STAKING HER CLAIM

The past held her hostage
Forming a hedge inhibiting sun
Fun became a stranger
And painful memories a warden
Limiting access to the present

And instead of her circle expanding
She found herself shrinking
Becoming smaller and smaller
Until the aggressor threatened to take her life

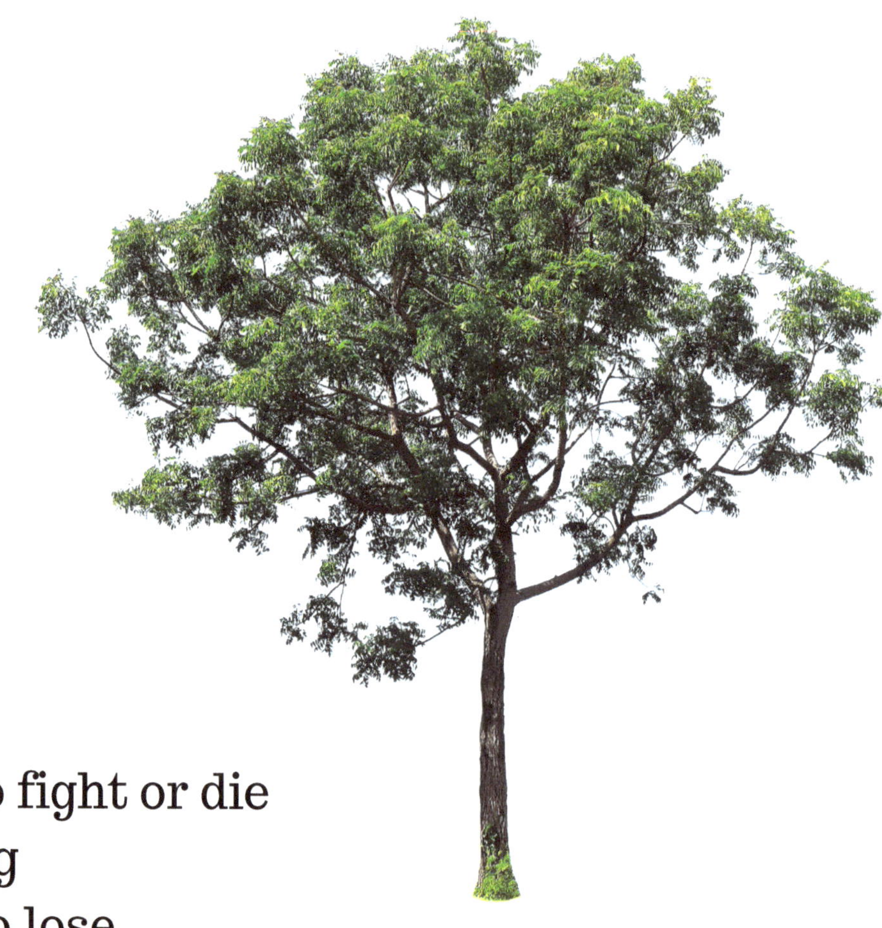

Left with the choice to fight or die
She came out swinging
For she had nothing to lose
And everything to gain
Saying goodbye to depression, rejection, and pain
By staking her claim to the tree of life

I BELIEVE YOU

WAITING FOR SUNRISE

In the darkness, I waited for sunrise ...
The time when the effects of hard days diminished
My hope was replenished
And I could finally see my way clearly

In Recovery

Disappointment held me down
And fenced me in
Swallowing my hopes for a season
I traveled a road watered with tears
And drank from a stream of longing
I sat at its bank

Trying to make sense of chaos
Collecting my thoughts
My heart stabilized, bypassing pain
Through open creative channels
I lie in recovery gaining strength-

One step closer to moving forward

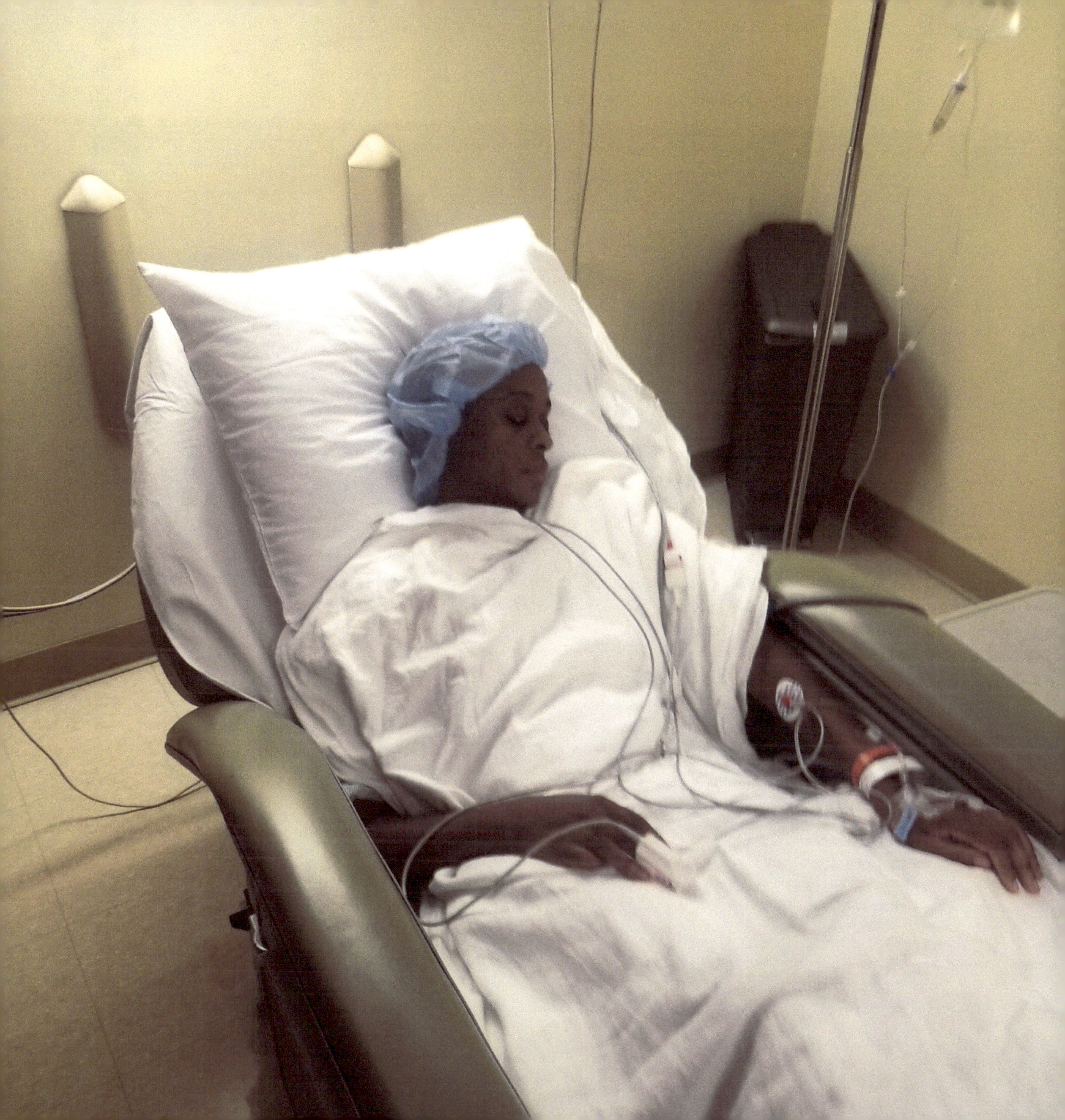

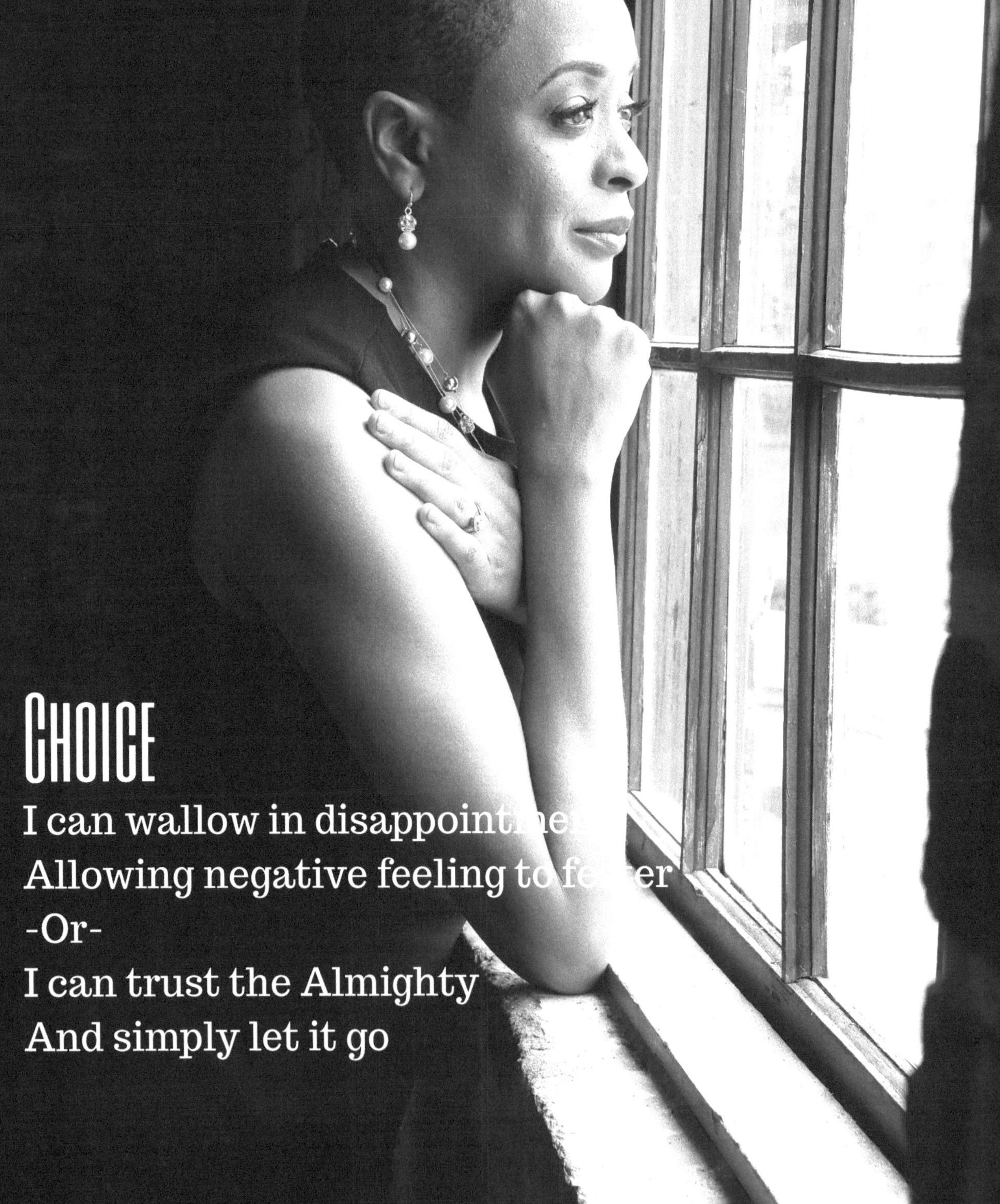
CHOICE
I can wallow in disappointment
Allowing negative feeling to fester
-Or-
I can trust the Almighty
And simply let it go

In retrospect

There are things He said
I decided not to hear
Words shared
I chose to ignore

Not because the content was strange
Or causing me pain
But because my heart wasn't ready
To receive this truth spoken

My open chambers broken
And not mended
So I pretended
I didn't hear what He said
But inside I really did

RESTORATIVE SPACE

His gift to me was space
And I moved in silence
Captivated by the stillness

Serenity doing its part
To restore torn and not mended
Finally transformed
Into a craftsman's work of art
Quietly set apart
Possessing a beauty that speaks volumes

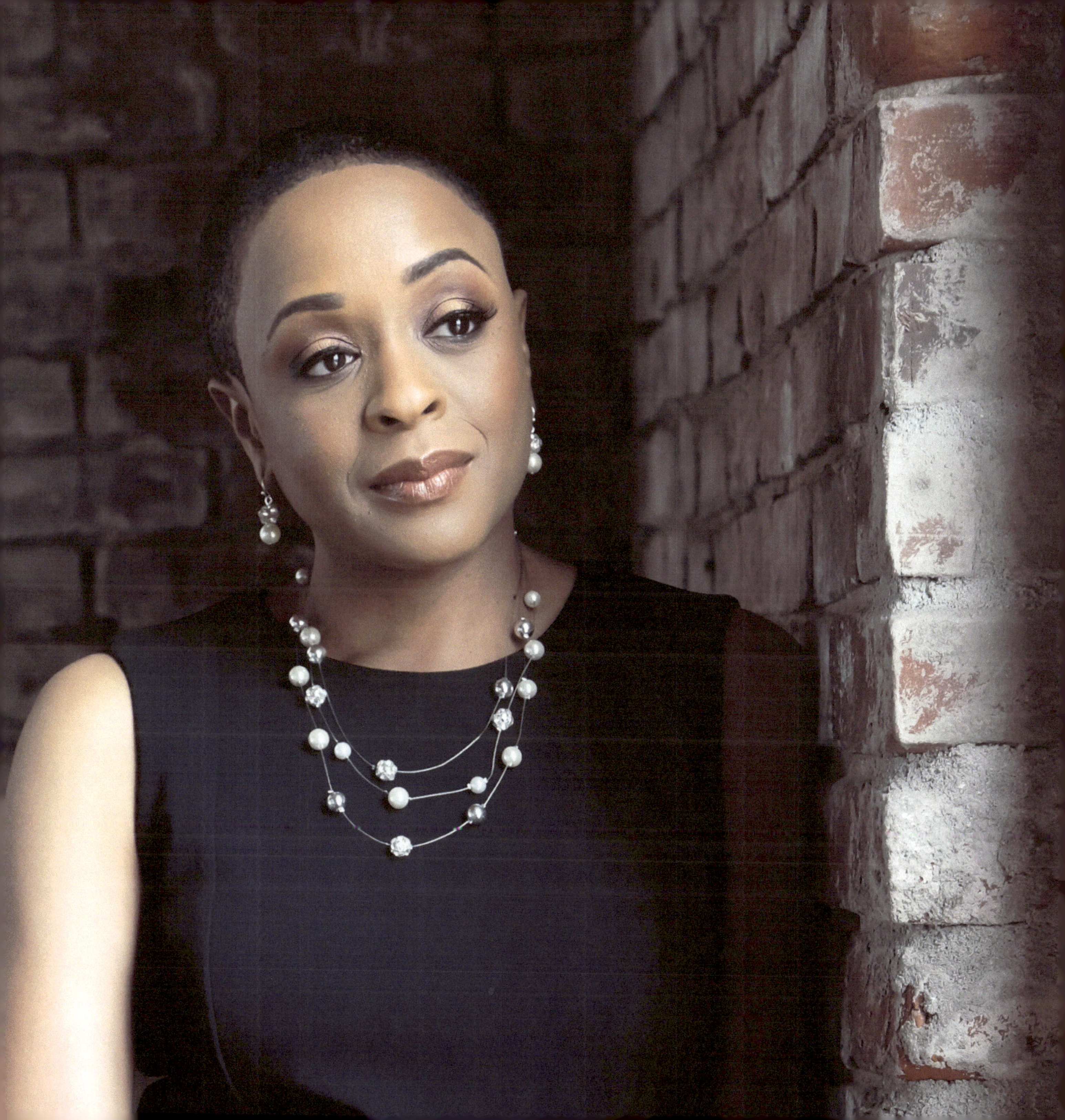

Flooding my soul

Warm love, calm love
Waves of goodness wash over me
I am filled with the presence

Of living love, enduring
Perfecting love, assuring
Healing love, curing

The broken, weak places in me Now my mind is completely free As I walk into destiny

MY ISHI

Before I rise
He quiets me with His love
Rejoicing over me with singing
I gratefully receive this gift
His generosity bringing joy
To a heart wide open

In that moment
Healing words gently spoken
Resurrect the dead
And mend broken fences
And unlock my defenses
And I bask in a Divine love
A source without end
And call Him
Husband, Lover, and Friend

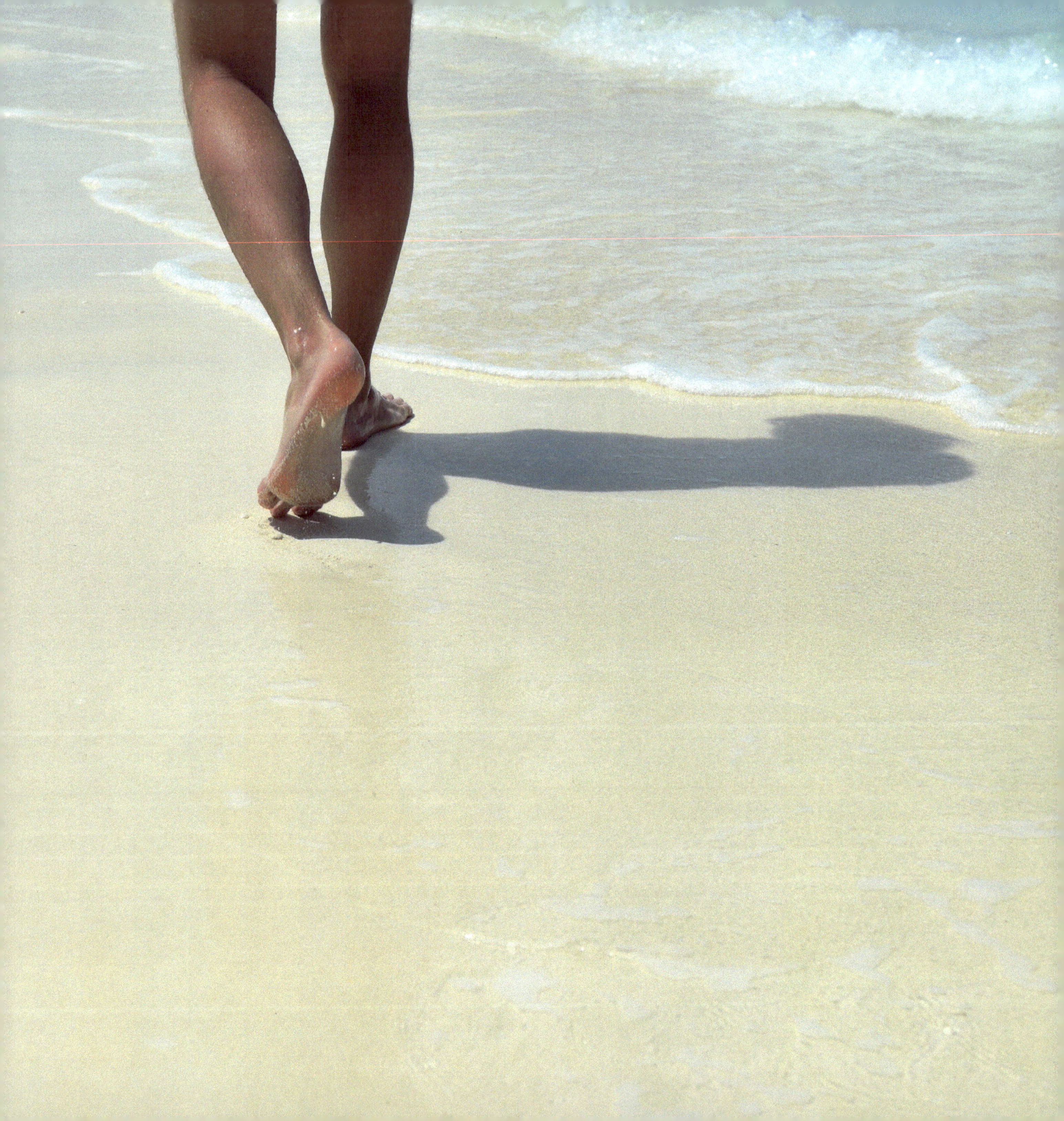

In the Cool of the Day

His voice holds my hand
And steadies my steps
As I walk in the stillness of His love

Time appears to cease
My harried movement suspended
And my heart becomes restful

As we walk side by side
I listen to the gentle wisdom
Flowing freely from His mouth

In the cool of the day,
I talk with God
And grow daily in knowledge and wisdom

Passion's Plea

Move me forward
Make my heart dance
And my belly ache
From laughter, not tears

As I surrender and release my fears
Flowing freely in the divine plan
Unhindered and uninterrupted
My life held firmly in God's hands

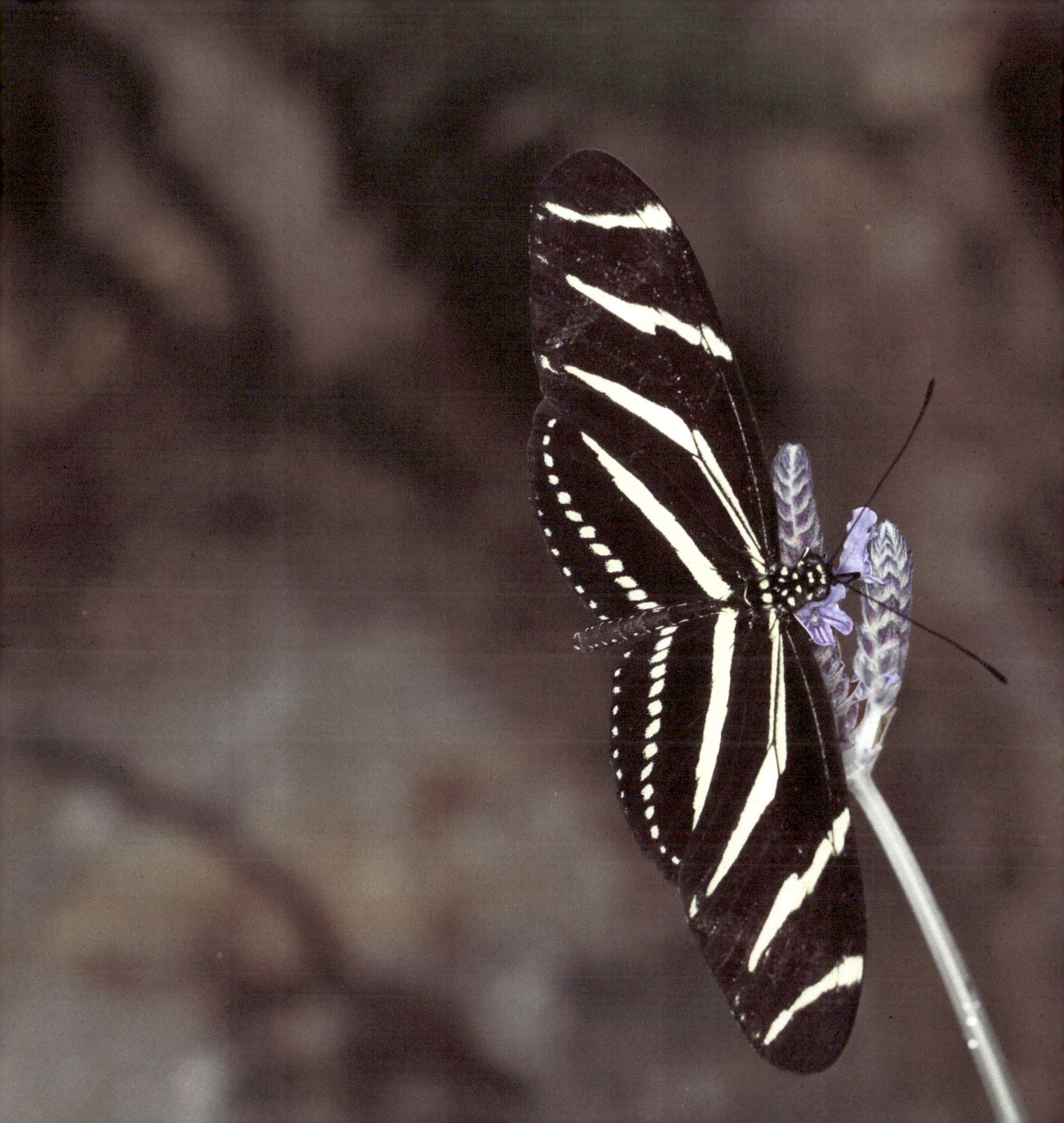

WAITING FOR SUNRISE

At 5am, the sky's a cobalt canvas
Completely devoid of light
I walk along the shoreline
Listening to the drifting of the ocean
The warm tide gently kissing my feet

The painted picture emerges slowly
Light and color added in subtle degrees
Observing the transitioning sky
One must possess a keen eye to recognize
And perceive the changes taking place

In the darkness you wait for sunrise
The time when the effect of nightfall is diminished
Light is replenished
And you can now see your way clearly

There's a tendency to want to rush the process
By closing your eyes and expecting the sky
To yield instant manifestation
But nature likes to take its time, quietly sublime
Yet never missing a single beat

In life, I've experienced a similar sequence
Of midnight preceding the dawn
Change emerged slowly with effects barely noticeable
My senses often dull to the transformation taking place
But I've found God faithful to complete His work in me

In the darkness, I waited for sunrise The time when the effects of hard days diminished
My hope was replenished And I could finally see my way clearly

Restoration

WHEN hurt took its last breath

JOY was instantly resurrected

PEACE was permanently established

FORGIVENESS reigned freely

STRENGTH returned from afar

PEACE was permanently established

AND GOD FINALLY HEALED THE LAND

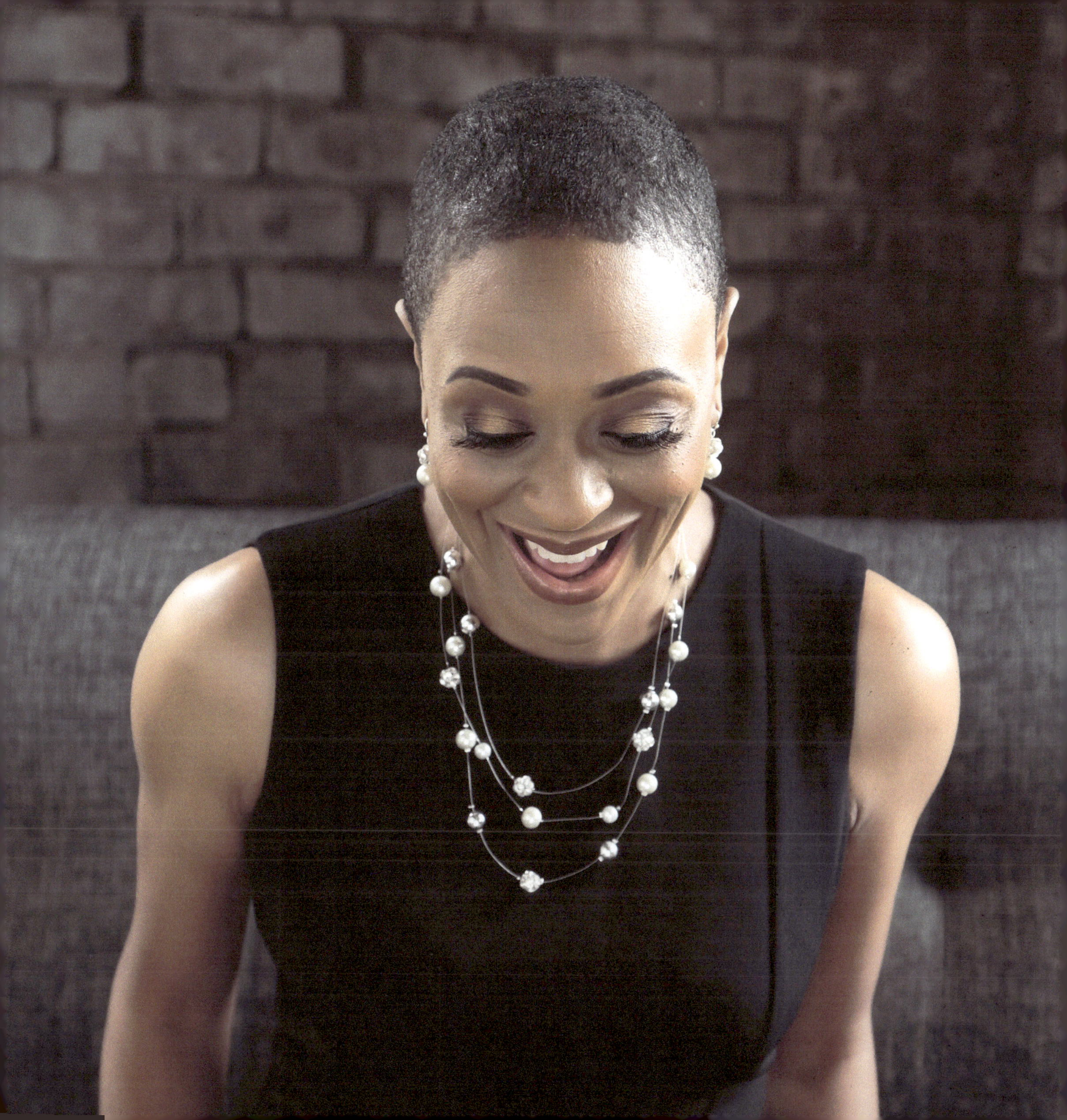

I BELIEVE YOU

Speaking Spirit

Open a mouth and the voice will speak ...
Open an ear and the heart will listen ...
Open a heart and unleash that soul's unlimited glory

Speaking Spirit

Left among the thorns
Beauty began to fade
Retreating deeper within

Great were the crimes
Committed against her land
But in silence
A greater injustice occurred-
Her voice failed to cry out

But Justice demands
That she must speak

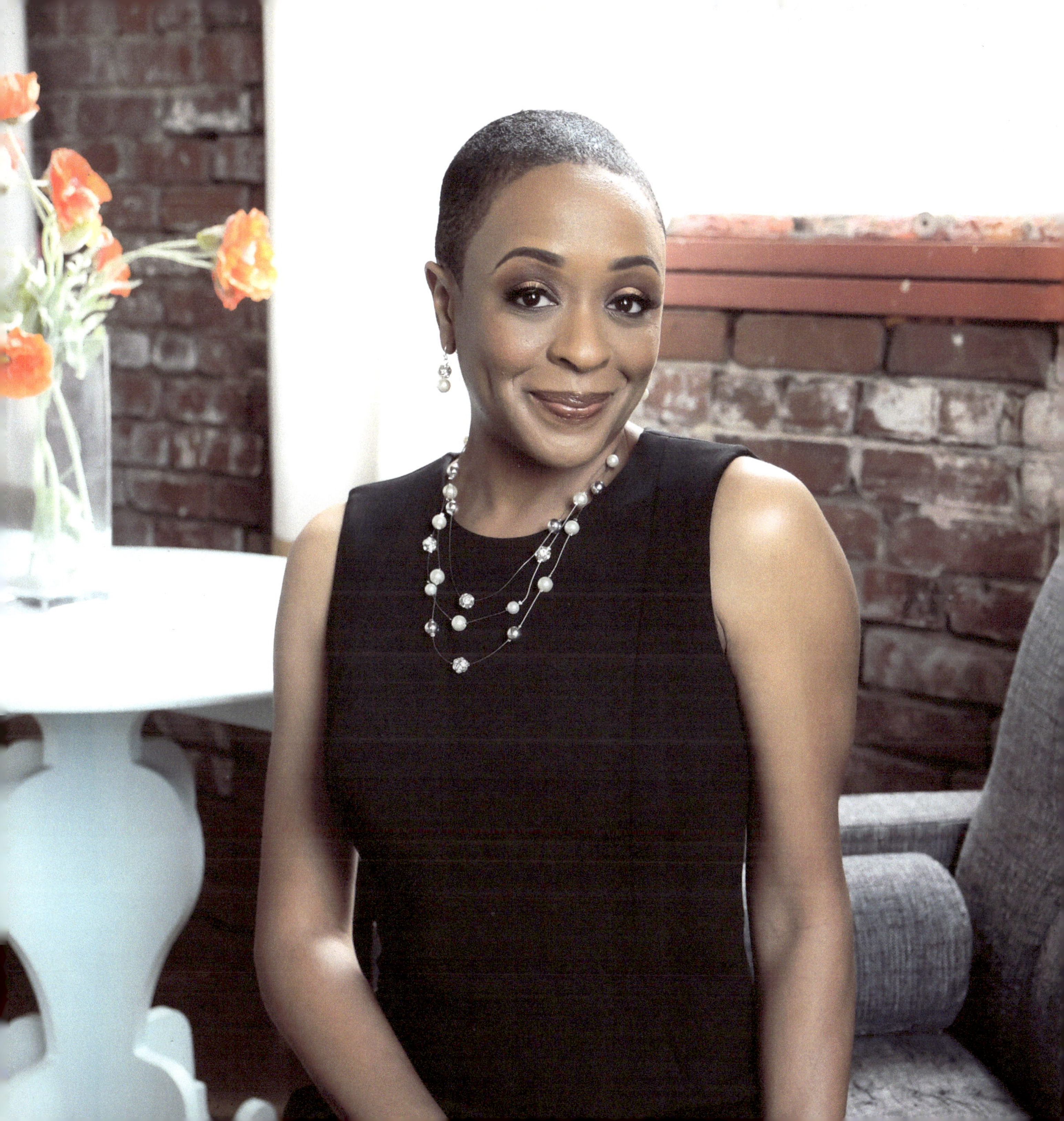

The Language of Tears

Tears shed have a voice
Articulated language filled
With adjectives and verbs Releasing pain
And subsequent healing

A cleansing expression
Sealed in a bottle
And written in a book
Documenting the exchange
Of weakness for strength

I BELIEVE YOU

SILENCE

HIDES VIOLENCE

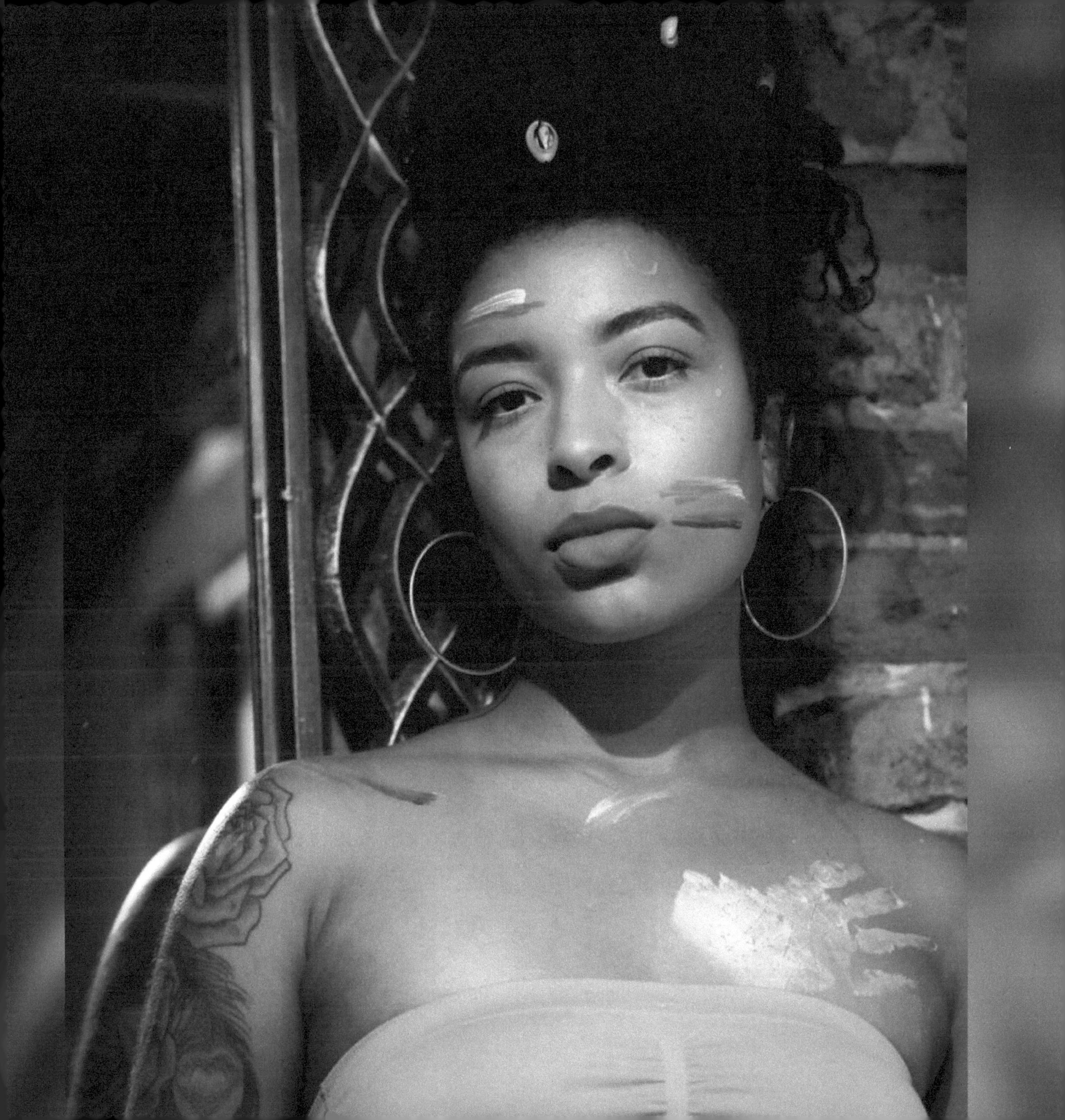

Breaking the Silence

Abuse buried in silence kills
Murdering the spirit of the victim
While enabling
The crime of the offender

Help comes from disclosure
The held captive set free
With vitality renewed and restored
Walking in victory

Choosing to F.L.Y. (finally love yourself)

Loving him
At the expense of YOU
Is not love
It is neglect

An unrighteous act
Demanding to be corrected

To all my sisters failing to love
Honor and cherish themselves

Repent and choose again

Time to let go
Relinquishing painful memories ...

Time to open up
To new possibilities ...

Time to move forward
Embracing your destiny ...

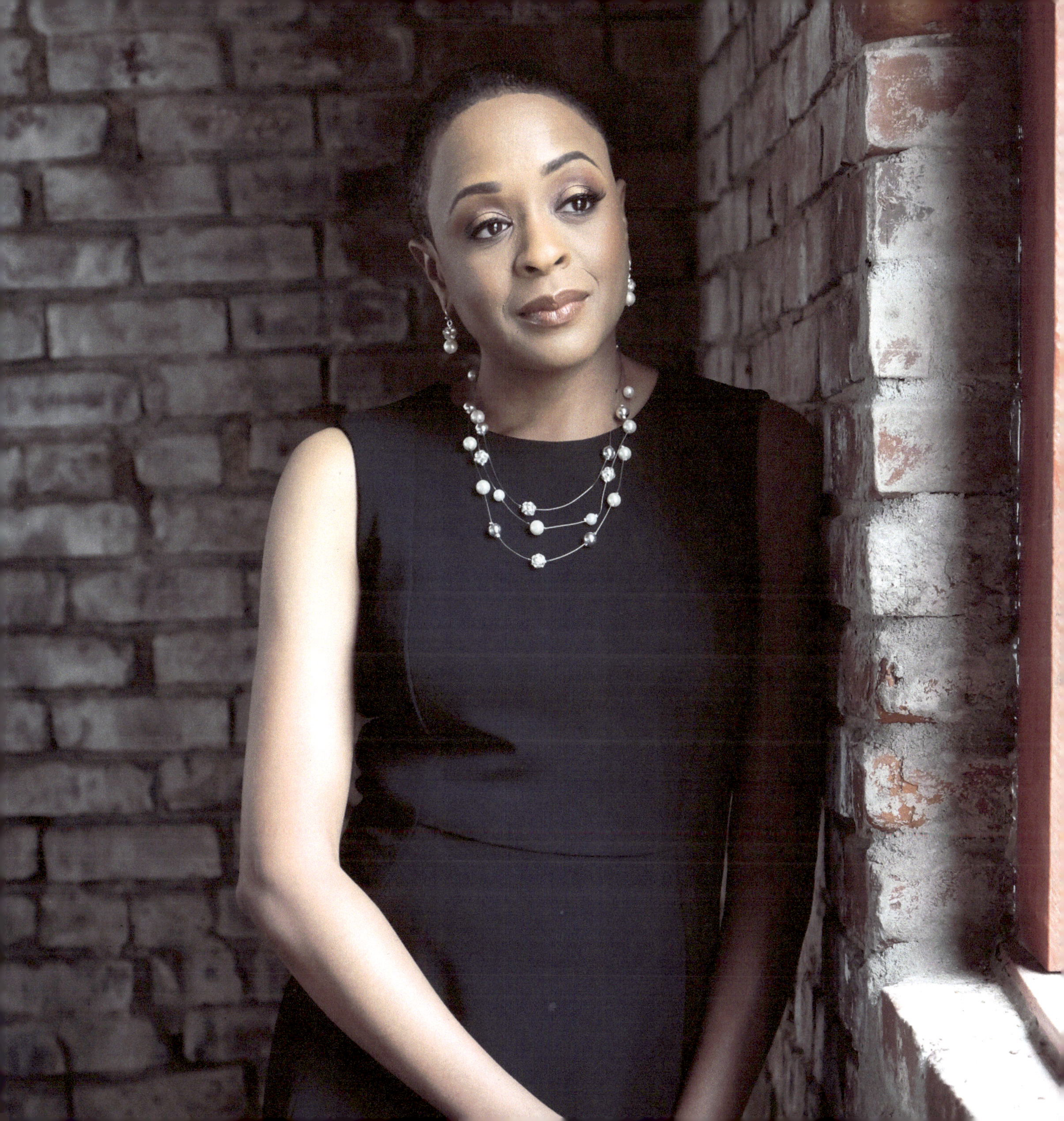

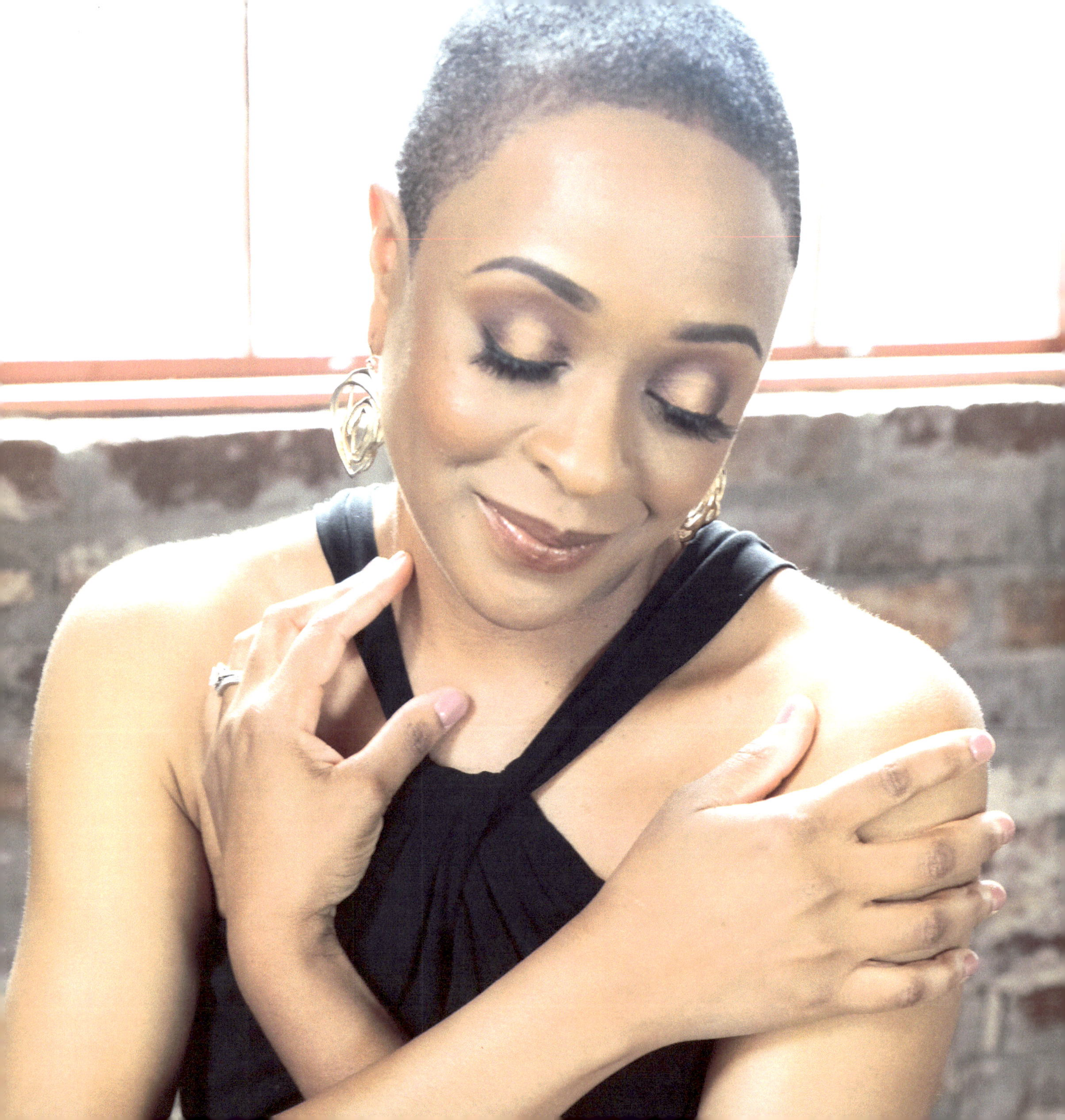

Daily Prayer

Help me be all You created me to be
A woman transformed
Pulling others from the storm
Living a life in full color

Go Forward

Go forward
Forget about standing still
Your destiny's true and real
Ready for you to grab it
With both hands
Possessing lands
You never knew existed

When depression comes, resist it
For God lovingly cares for you
Holding you securely in His hands
And in His strength you can stand
And run free

Because His love never fails

CONTINUATION ST

Dare to live again
Dare to dream again
Creating now moments
Proud moments
Shared with friends

Celebrating the choice
To freely love again

Independence Day

I opened the blind
And receiving the light
Darkness came undone

Gazing upon green pasture
I left trouble waters
Fear fleeing in the face of possiblity

Capacity Filled

The past stood knocking at my door
As was instructed
To read the posted sign

PLEASE DO NOT DISTURB
THERE IS NO ROOM IN THE INN
IN THE PRESENT
I AM FILLED TO CAPACITY

(singing)
New time, new day
Left behind the old way

Forward Motion

My past has tried unsuccessfully
To rob me of my present

My present beauty, my present joy
And my current creative moments

By attempting to turn my gaze backward
Into the abyss of moments already lived

When whispering voices summon me
To resurrect the dead, I quickly remind myself
That the buried, decaying things in my life
Must stay in the ground to provide fuel for future harvests
I give no territory to what has transpired before

For life only unfurls with forward motion

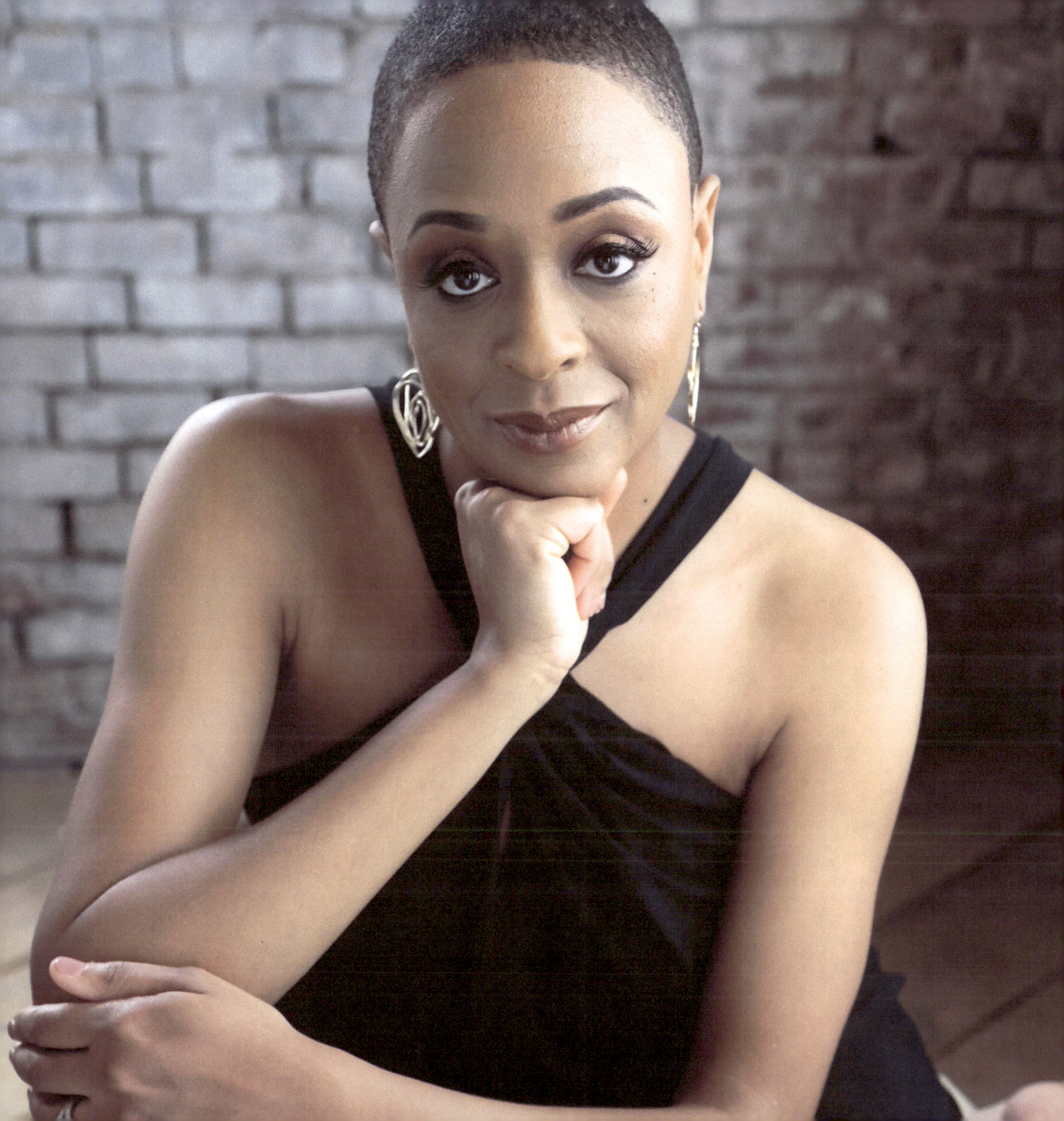

Living Bundle (Part 1)

I may encounter things
Sent to confuse me
Circumstances
Trying to depress me
By spirits
Attempting to harass me
But of one thing I am sure

None of this mess will move me
Stress me
Or even possess me
For my life is bound tightly
As a living bundle
And In God's hands
I am always secure

Living Bundle (Part 2)

Never leaving my side
I turn and You're there
Always ready to share
The special love You have for me

Your love is like a blanket
I wrap myself in
Leaving my snuggly warm
And forever drawn
To its cushiony comfort

In Your arms I rest like a baby
And find myself bound
As a living bundle
In the care of my God

Good News

Release negativity
Those things that cause you stress
Embrace only positive energy
And let God handle the rest
My friend good things await you
So there's no need to fret
Emmanuel's got it all in His hands
And He's not through with you yet

Speak your goodness into existence
For every word has Power
In trying times find refuge
In His everlasting tower
Of Love, Peace, Strength, Mercy
Whatever you need it's there
And remember, the answers
To life's unsolvable mysteries
Are often found through prayer

I BELIEVE YOU

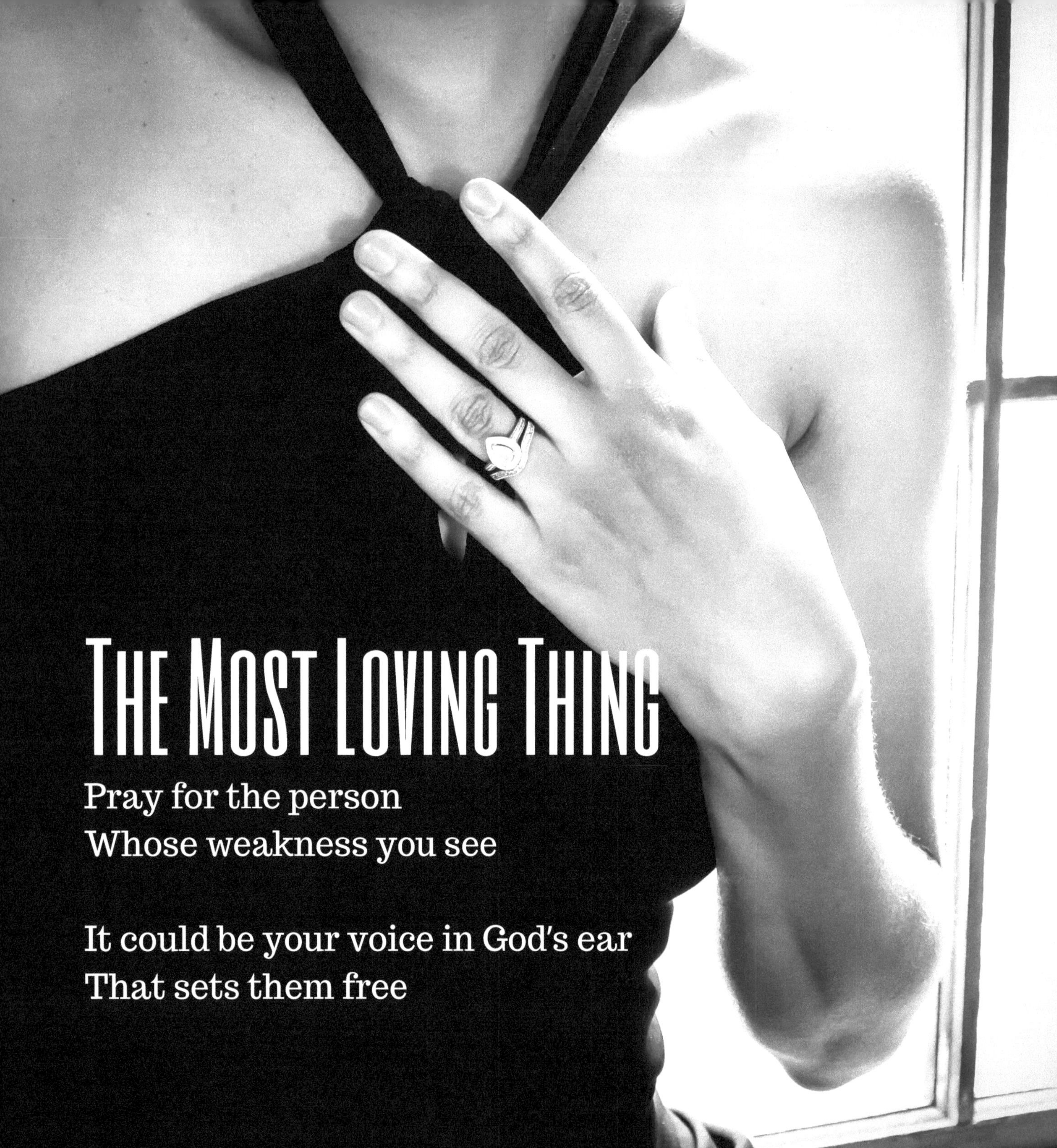
THE MOST LOVING THING
Pray for the person
Whose weakness you see
It could be your voice in God's ear
That sets them free

Deciding Daily

Forgiveness is a decision
I must choose everyday
Because misunderstanding
Always stands lurking
Ready to seize
Any presented opportunity

But Humility closes the gap
Building a bridge
Over troubled water
And Love seals the deal
Making the rough places
Smooth again

Breaking Alabaster

Letting love flow freely
Is no easy task especially
When another's actions
Contribute to disharmony
Whether intentional or not

But to choose not to flow
Would be a greater injustice
So, in spite of the opposition
I find myself breaking alabaster
And on my knees finding peace

The Most Loving Thing

In response to injustice
And outcry is raised
One that may be politically incorrect
By certainly heartfelt

But what should happen
When the oppressor
Turns a deaf ear
Fails to take responsibility for the action
And charges the injured party with a crime

Sometimes the most loving thing
Is choosing not to hate

Billy Buck

His heart held pain until it festered
Rotted and polluted his thinking
Turning his life towards the path
That led to death and destruction

The tragedy being, he never realized
The course he had chosen
For he believed fury make him strong
Allowing him to defeat his enemies

I wept when I encountered his presence
For I could see the beauty lying dormant beneath
His eyes a reflection of a hurting humanity
I spoke life to his decaying form

And saw a young man walk on water

I BELIEVE YOU

The Beauty Within

Whether we know it or not
Every person is fighting their own battle
But compassion must extend itself
Beyond personal struggle
To embrace the needs of another

When this happens, everyone's load is lifted

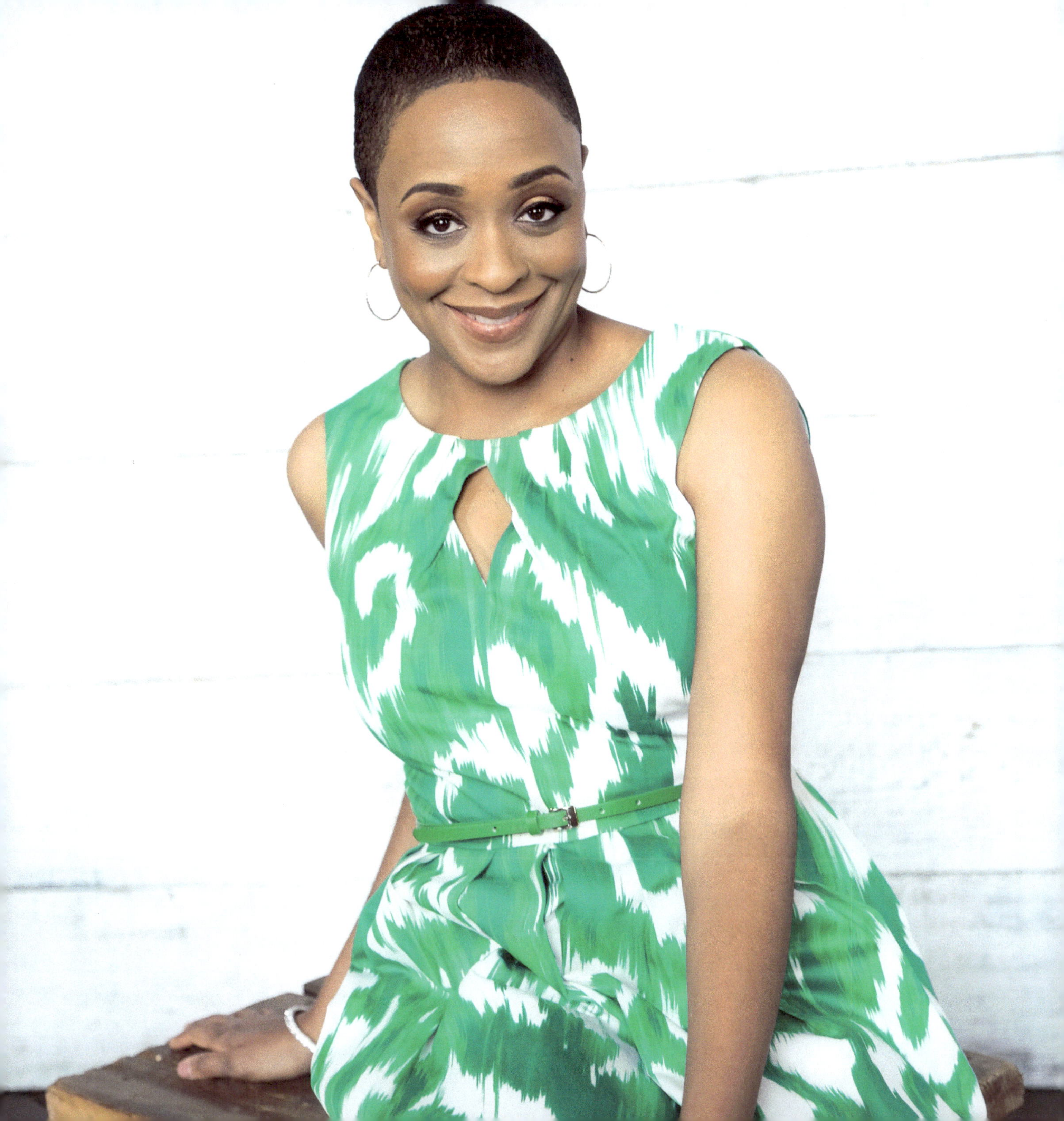

Prima Donna

"Prima Donna" is Italian for "First Lady"

In modern times,
Language is often distorted
And the original
Meaning of words lost
But if actions truly define character
Bad should mean bad
And good should mean good

Men have often envied and feared
The freedom observed in another
Without realizing
That liberty has a high cost
It is born in sacrifice and in pain
Late nights
While others partake of slumber

Courage under fire
And sheer determination against
Seemingly insurmountable odds

I will not let the actions of another
Rob me of the essence
Of the true Prima Donna
For based on the original definition
It invokes in my mind
The vision of a woman
With character and integrity
Beauty and strength
Qualities worthy of admiration
And certainly not fear

God saw beauty in the face
Of this Prima Donna
Who are you
To undermine His glory?

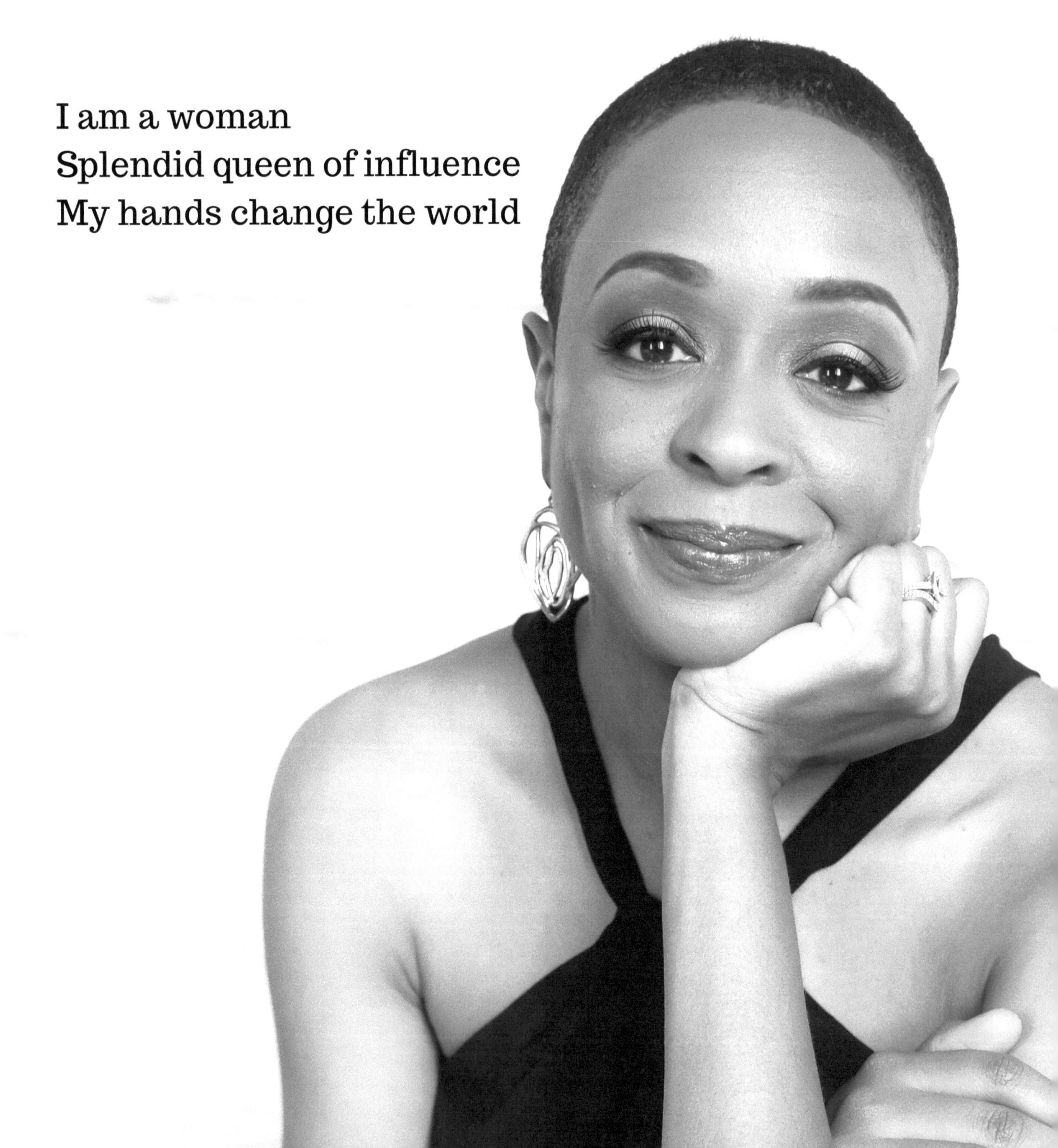
I am a woman
Splendid queen of influence
My hands change the world

Nikki in the Garden

I regurgitate the lie
That says that I have to be

busy...to be productive
busy...to be significant
busy...to leave a permanent mark on the world

So, today I

stop...to smell the roses
and enjoy...the children's laughter
while thanking God...for the marvelous gift
of creation

Here in the pauses are my most significant moments

A Laying on of Words

Ms. Lady,

It's been too long since we last spoke. Precious moments have elapsed minus the necessary communication common among sister-friends. Have you been told lately how amazing, gifted, beautiful, and valued you are? If not, pause for a moment and observe your reflection through the mirror of another's eyes.

I see greatness just waiting to be unleashed- God-given ability to turn and change the world, deposited and hidden inside for safekeeping. Permit me to summon forth every dormant gift.

Your treasure is no longer allowed to remain buried and idle, but instead released with the commission to prosper and multiply. You are blessed to be a blessing. Act as such, so when our giftedness meets again, the earth will not be able to contain the collective glory.

Woman, know that you are appreciated and loved simply because God took the time to plant you in the earth. Don't allow anyone to steal your thunder, especially when they haven't eyes to appreciate the beauty of creation.

Keep the soil of your heart on reserve for the farmer ready to plant life-giving, healthy vegetation, and not the interloper carelessly scattering weeds. Guard your ground with all diligence, for from it will come the substance of your life.

May these words empower and keep you, strengthen and sustain you, and forever remind you of who you really are.

Love,

Chanel

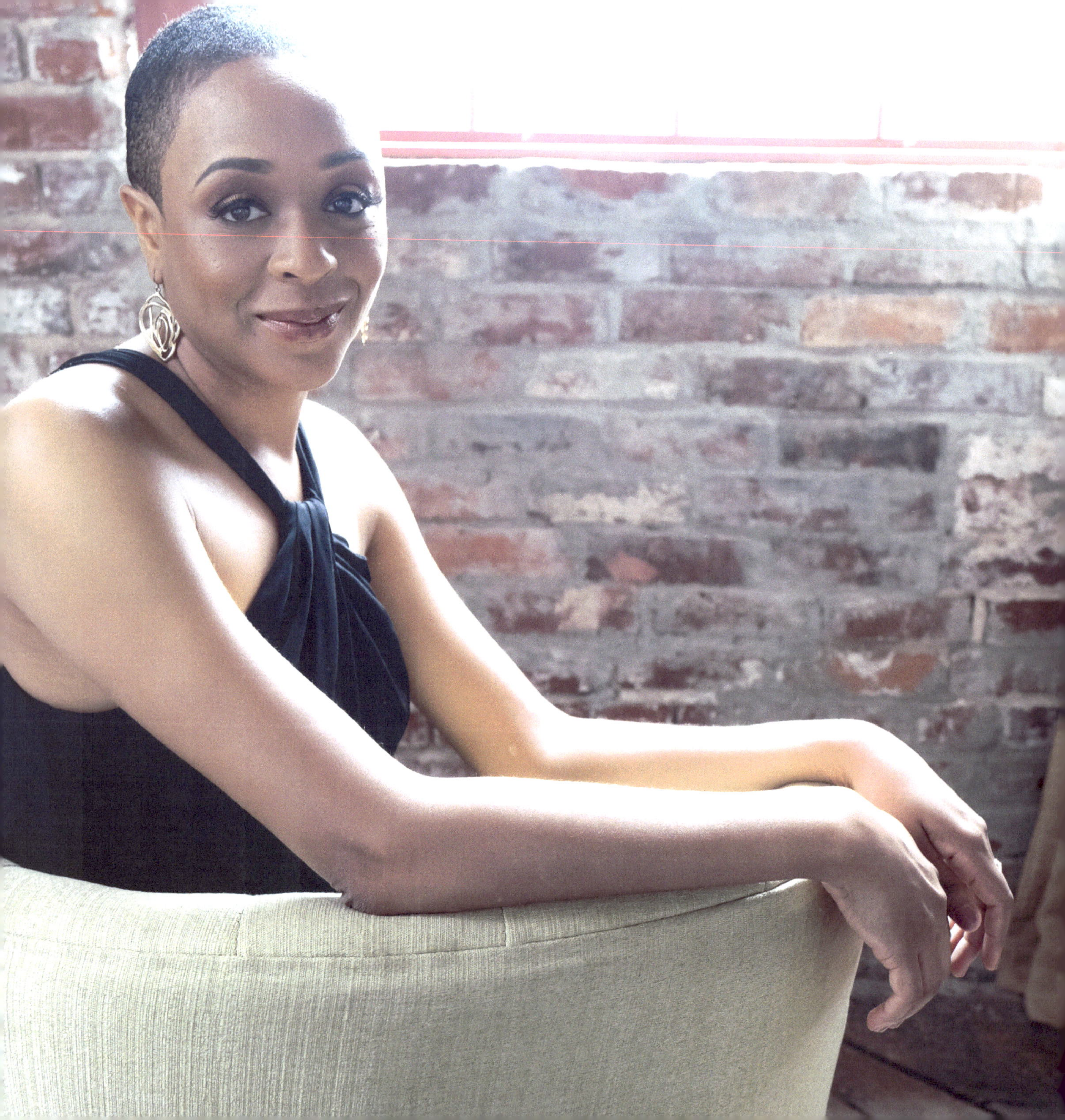

Step inside a place of delight
Far removed
From the stress of the world
Breathe deeply
Releasing the cares of the day
And find rest by the peaceful streams

Be still and let the whispering
Breezes speak gently to your spirit
These are words you must hear
Listen carefully and live

Worlds are formed and fashioned
By a voice
Loaded with the spoken word
Conception begins in the heart
And when released with the mouth
Gives birth of the unseen
Into the visible realm
Words create everything that is seen

Speak beauty
To the deserted, ruined places
And watch abundant life
Suddenly spring forth
Where there is confusion
Disorder and chaos
Cry out "Peace be still"
And watch
The thundering waves cease

To confront hopelessness
Summon words of encouragement
And watch faith walk on water
A feat only dirt believes impossible
But know that dirt belongs
Under your feet
And if thrown in your face

Quickly return it to its proper place
A garden permits
Whatever is sown in it to come forth
So continue to plant well
The beauty and favor of the Lord
Is upon you
And it is marvelous in our eyes

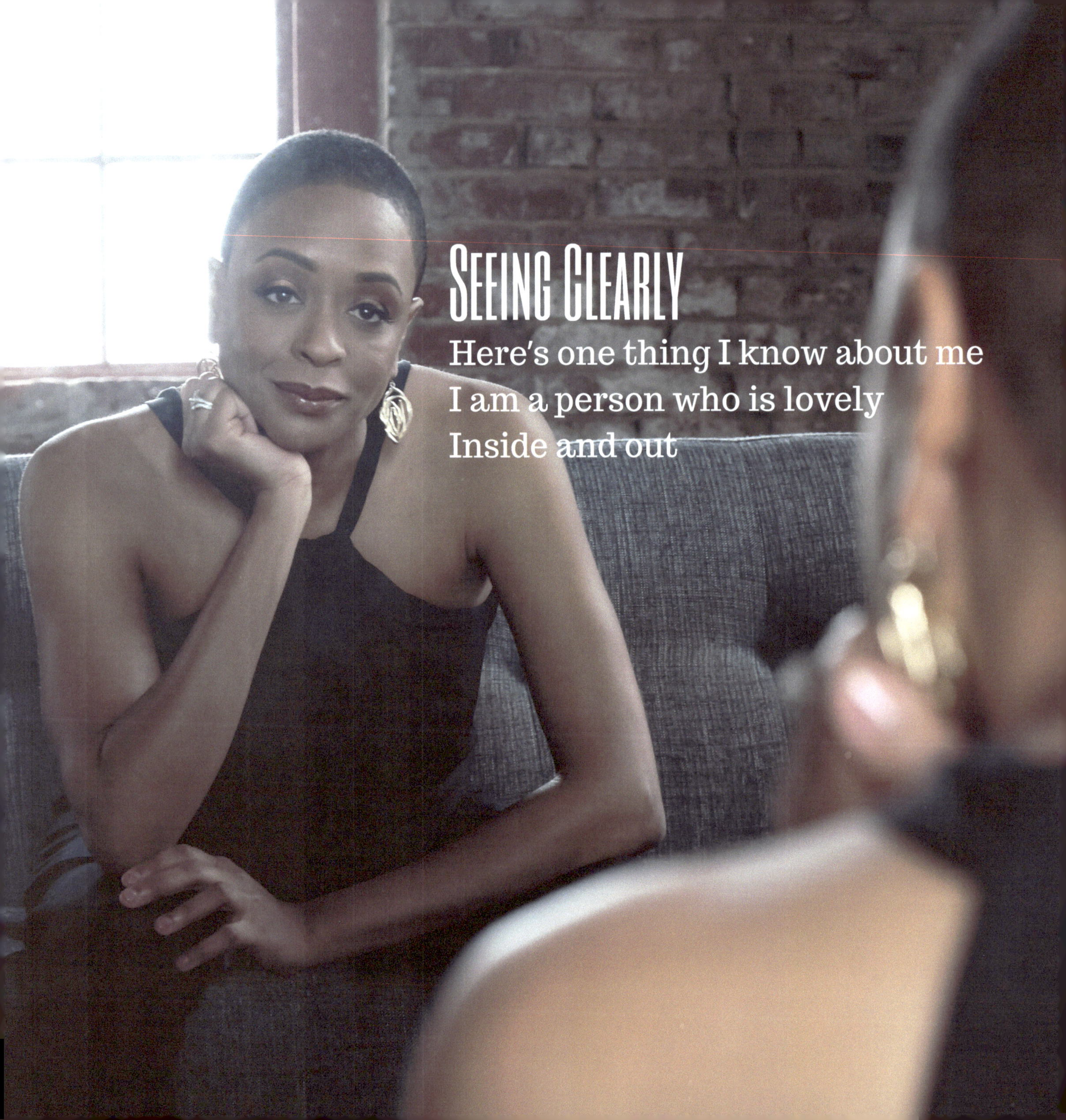
SEEING CLEARLY
Here's one thing I know about me
I am a person who is lovely
Inside and out

Testament of My Faith

I'll find a way to love

No matter what happens
Or what painful event occurs
As long as there is breath
And I am breathing

I'll find a way to love

Living Love

While I'm living
I'll love myself
And other human beings
Created in the image of God

When I love I'm living, breathing
Undeniable proof
Of a loving, living God

The Beauty of My Life

The beauty of my life ...
Is not that I did everything right
The truth is ...
I made a lot of mistakes
But when faced with what looked like disaster
I kept going
I kept breathing
I kept living

And giving God my hand
I pushed past pain
Rediscovering Beauty
Reclaiming Joy
Finding Goodness

In myself and in others

Tribulation didn't destroy me ...
That is the beauty of my life

Hephzibah: My Delight is in Her

Conquering woman of faith
Having no doubt that the word of God will surely come to pass
Aggressively, she steps out in faith
Not seeking her own will
Endeavoring only to do the will and pleasure of the Father
Love overflows within her

Running over to the point that
Yokes, burdens, and all plots of the wicked one
Are annihilated with the kindness of her lips
Nothing can ever separate her from Me

I BELIEVE YOU

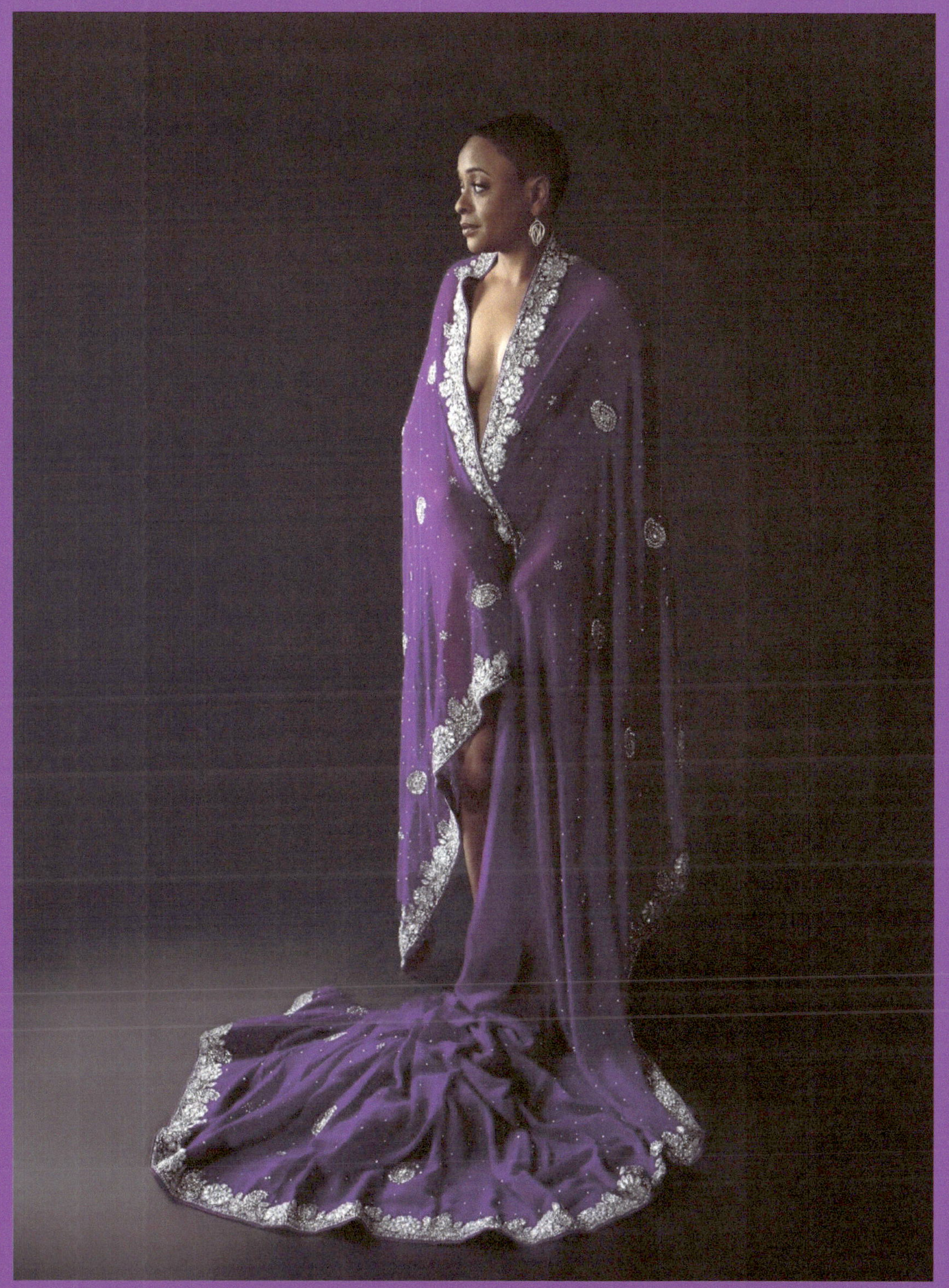

Chanel Nicole Ryan

AUTHOR. CREATIVE. ADVOCATE. COACH.

Atlanta based photographer and creative writer, Chanel Nicole Ryan uses her lens and pen to tell the stories of humanity. Her creative endeavors and personal experiences have culminated in her debut title, THINGS SAID - A COLLECTION OF HEALING WORDS FOR THE SOUL. Shedding light on the dark place of domestic violence, Chanel is the creator of The Purple Warrior Project, a community of survivors and advocates.

Chanel holds a Doctor of Pharmacy degree from Florida A & M University. She is a trauma recovery coach, specializing in grief, loss, and betrayal. Chanel is the proud mother of one son, Eli.

www.ingramcontent.com/pod-product-compliance
Lightning Source LLC
LaVergne TN
LVHW070217110826
845147LV00003B/594

* 9 7 8 0 9 9 8 9 9 4 5 9 8 *